FRENEMY TYRANT

Written and illustrated by

Karen Kellock Ph.D.

Manual for Superior Men

This is a complete theory based on Einstein physics, Political Psychology, Systems Theory and Archetypal Psychiatry.

FORMULA

All success attraction
All disease obstruction
All recovery elimination

You must fast on all three

OBSTRUCTIONS:

People
Habit
Food

FRENEMY TYRANT

Trust ye not in a friend, put no confidence in a guide: a man's enemies are in his own home beside. By being rejected and sequestered you built character and they didn't: born with a silver spoon = idiots. She's on your turf competing with you. That's just her script but what is she doing there, fool? Why be so involved socially--people die or move away. Then all that time invested, for what I say? Don't feel empty cuz you're lonely, separation means HOLY and now God showers you with the lovely. Stop feeling remorse over past sins repented of--He doesn't wanna hear about such things love.

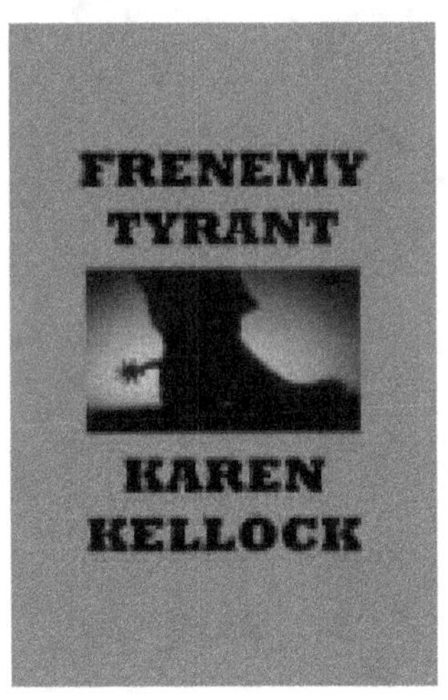

YOU ROSE BACK UP

TOXIC IMPACTS OF DISRESPECT
GAMEPLAYING IS DISRESPECT
DON'T CONVINCE EM, SHOW EM
SETTLING FOR LESS
THEY WERE UNWILLING TO BEGIN WITH
NEVER APOLOGIZE FOR BOUNDARIES
HE THINKS BREADCRUMBS ARE ENOUGH
HE KNOWS SHE'LL COME BACK
NEVER SETTLE FOR CRUMBS
FRENEMIES WANT YOUR MONEY
DON'T TELL EM ABOUT YOUR WINDFALL
IT'S NOT THAT YOUR STINGY
YOUR HARD WORK BRINGS HATE TOO
YOU HIT BOTTOM AND CAME BACK
IT ALL HAD TO HAPPEN AS IT DID

YOU ROSE BACK UP

TOXIC IMPACTS OF DISRESPECT

Intentions don't matter when the impact is toxic. Silence allows it and that's what keeps you sick.

Here's the system Sue: When people disrespect you, silence gives them permission to continue.

The next time he cancels plans without warning simply say "I deserve one who values my time" ok.

Ask yourself: why am I giving so much to one who gives so little? That will change your life on the double.

The person who's irreplaceable in life is yourself, not him/her. That stops the chase, a bummer.

You're leaning on an old wobbly chair thinking it's a high building. Suddenly you wake up and it's thrilling.

He thinks he's the best she could ever have, that's why he treats her like that: what a dam brat!

GAMEPLAYING IS DISRESPECT

Any man who plays games disrespects your time and mind. Getting em back makes you refined.

As soon as you see they're **NOT** the prize you'll see what I saw: you've been letting em dim your light.

What if you fear empty without em? That's the fear they're counting on, that's the whole game hon'.

He's made you an empty shell and **THAT'S** why you need him--like hell! Get smart, say farewell.

YOU ROSE BACK UP

The emptiness felt from his absence is the space you can now fill with your talents and progress.

That created space is your FREEDOM, your peace and potential. How exciting focusing on the essential.

DON'T CONVINCE EM, SHOW EM

You don't convince em of their replaceability, you show em with actions by focusing on yourself see.

The man who truly deserves you will never make you question your worth, time or value.

The arrogant man is just your stepping stone or placeholder to your life around the corner.

The woman knowing her worth doesn't chase, beg or settle. She rises and reigns, that is all.

The queen leaves those who underestimated her in the dust. She never thinks of em again, or bust!

Lesson: When she accepts less than she deserves, she teaches him that's all he needs to give her.

Every single time you adjust your life to suit their convenience, you lower your standards see.

When they pull back when you need em most, they're watching to see what you'll do, then adjust.

SETTLING FOR LESS

Will you walk away or stay, accepting less? This is how the game works so don't be blind Lass.

He tramples through her garden smashing the flowers without ever watering it. And she settles for it?

YOU ROSE BACK UP

The right person will rise to meet your standards & not complain about it. Never settle or regret it.

Wrong people will say you're asking for the impossible, wanting to keep you quiet/under control.

What if raising your standards means you lose him? That's exactly the point, do it now friend!

Any man who can't meet your standards doesn't deserve your presence. That's the essence.

THEY WERE UNWILLING TO BEGIN WITH

If he's unwilling to step up then he was never truly hers to begin with. That's how the queen sees it

How to raise your standards: decide right now what you will and will not tolerate, despite his words.

With every boundary enforced your confidence grows. Raising standards honors herself you know.

As you stand taller he weight of settling begins to fall away and it's a bright new beautiful day.

Settling bloats the cheeks and you look like a chipmunk see. Now slim down to elegance, released!

Of course he'll test you to see if you really mean it. Keep those boundaries and self-worth, believe it.

NEVER APOLOGIZE FOR BOUNDARIES

Never apologize for boundaries or explain why you deserve em see. That alone shows you're unfree.

When he can't rise to meet your standards, let em go. It needs no more discussion you know.

YOU ROSE BACK UP

Repeat after me: My standards are my crown and I wear it proudly. No explanation is needed honey.

Raise your standards so high only those who truly deserve you can reach em: that's key friends.

Those who refuse to settle don't just find love, they find themselves and that's the highest of all.

HE THINKS BREADCRUMBS ARE ENOUGH

If he thinks his breadcrumbs are enough, starve him out. Stand up against his tyranny, excuses & fluff.

A man giving you breadcrumbs isn't feeding his soul, he's feeding his ego and living very low.

When you stop taking his breadcrumbs, he starves. Reach your breaking point, see the stars!

For years she lived on scraps of attention. A complement here/fleeting kindness there: bummer!

Every time she saw things improving he'd pull back, leaving her hungry for more, feeling lack.

Breadcrumbs aren't an accident, they're a strategy. Men like him don't give just enough, not blindly.

He gives enough to keep you invested & doubt your worth. It makes me sick what they do to girls.

HE KNOWS SHE'LL COME BACK

He knows she'll come back to little pieces of affection so manipulates her to stay this way.

In his mind he didn't believe she felt she deserved the whole loaf. It's really a disgusting approach.

YOU ROSE BACK UP

Why be afraid of losing one who'se already shown you they're not going to give? Don't go back/relive.

The love you deserve isn't something you have to beg for. Imagine that scenario, what a bummer!

If he walks away, let him. It's not your loss but your freedom. Can you take it back then some?

No need to play hard to get. Your silence speaks louder than any words--see this and you're all set.

NEVER SETTLE FOR CRUMBS

Never settle for crumbs when you deserve the feast. Say that and say it again, reject that beast.

Any man giving breadcrumbs thinks you'll keep coming back but when you stop the game ends Mack.

You used to party with these people until you started prospering then you became a frenemy see.

Stop telling bad spirits good news cuz they'll just wanna borrow from you then you're back in the blues.

Why do the rich hang with the rich? Cuz the poor will gouge you to death begging from the ditch.

God blessed YOU from making good choices--not them--but they feel entitled to it friend.

You get a windfall cuz God is pleased and the sleaze feel entitled to some of it: that's how it's perceived.

Stay away from people who benefited from you but act like you never gave them anything too.

FRENEMIES WANT YOUR MONEY

YOU ROSE BACK UP

If blessed by God frenemies come around wanting a certain percentage. That's just the way it is.

Never tell bad spirits good news or they'll be around for their cut and anything else you have too.

It's never been so hard holding on to money since you're surrounded by beggars friends & family.

DON'T TELL EM ABOUT YOUR WINDFALL

Don't ever tell them you got a windfall or they'll instantly start planning how to get some or all.

Beggars ask for food or money without reciprocity. Also small things--got a cigarette honey?

When you're rich they all wanna get close to you. Get smart: hang with rich-- they won't beg you too.

A food brags of his money but a shrewd one keeps it secret because it saves him trouble see.

Learning about people and these foibles is your most valuable lesson which will save you double.

Not only do they want your money they wanna move in and take your sanity or anything else within.

To be all-knowing, be suspicious of people ESPECIALLY those deemed to be good, wise or loving.

IT'S NOT THAT YOUR STINGY

When she asked me for my money it wasn't that I was greedy but I saw her for the first time see.

Other words for it: sponger, moocher, freeloader and gigolo. These are all disgusting you know.

YOU ROSE BACK UP

We are to judge people on the content of their character not DEI which is nothing but a bummer.

When they come at you as a supporting angel but you know they're a snake in your garden, careful.

The chosen ones are rising this season and people's true colors are coming out for this reason.

YOUR HARD WORK BRINGS HATE TOO

You think after all your hard work they'll finally like you? Forget it, they'll hate you more for success Sue.

It's not that you're good but you're doing better than them. That's when their energy changes friend.

When you come to a totally new level you'll feel awkward around old, that's how you know.

The more fake you are, the bigger your circle. The more real you are, the smaller: that's how it is girl.

Real ones with divine energy will be lucky to have ONE friend. It's hard to believe but true, amen?

YOU HIT BOTTOM AND CAME BACK

You hit rock bottom then came back ON YOUR OWN. Just that is a tremendous feat you know.

You were mocked, misjudged, scorned & hated--just as happens to all the chosen--but still made it.

What happened to you no one else could have taken. It made you strong being so forlorned and hated.

You literally went through hell while on earth, shattering all delusions while all the fakers came first.

YOU ROSE BACK UP

You were shattered when people you trusted raised their heel against you, scared to death too.

Now you shine as a bright light as God's given you double for your trouble. What a life, on top now.

Now you know how to lead, having been on the bottom spat upon like a grasshopper under their feet.

IT ALL HAD TO HAPPEN AS IT DID

This all had to happen: you were just that naive. You didn't know about people and sinned to relieve.

All this abuse you took made you warm steel, a velvet glove. You have empathy with love from above.

Now you're on top, a handsome leader of the flock. You've learned the ropes from Karen kellock.

People are cruel and the "nice" are the cruelest. You could only learn this from your messes.

AUTHOR'S NOTE

Celebrate what's about to happen. You don't know what it is but can feel the seasons changin'.

To compete in his stable is degrading and humiliating. To be queenly just stay the hell away lady.

People come and go, the answer is to go within. This makes you magnetic attracting mass followin'

He did not know how I should be treated cuz I did not know but what I do know: it gave me IBS.

Because I was clean, orderly and decent I assumed others were: I needed street education.

Focus on you because people come and go. People worship is idolatry and comes from below.

The things that break your heart will fix your vision and that is a rocket launcher to a new life son.

Loneliness is the price you pay for self-improvement. What does that say about envy of humans?

Be kind but don't let em use you. Be warm steel, using the velvet glove approach but sweet too.

Some people make you feel lonely. Stay away: no company is better than bad ones honey.

Stay patient, for the best things happen unexpectedly. Chance favors a prepared mind SUDDENLY.

Normalize walking alone cuz your goals are personal and people hold you down [you're versatile].

The family you create is more important than the one you came from. This relieves more than some.

Author's Note

Those who express individuality in their attire are subject to public shaming. North Korea

Can there be fun and hope in the desert of oppression? Not so much, it's excruciating with this person.

He's so despicably shallow--lost in meaningless detail--I wonder: why do you want him girl?

We're born sovereign but then made to conform. Made to accept crap til we can't: that's conversion.

Just by going there you are competing in his petty little stable so I'll say it again: quit it Mabel.

After the bedlam in Normandy 1945 it is utter beauty and calm. It's always triumph after tribulation.

Stop stuffing information from the outside in and increase your amplitude: listen within.

Simplicity in words shows guts and self-assurance but only a discoverer can do that with coherence.

I've already unified opposites/resolved all contradictions, I don't need image magicians.

Carnivore Diet: It's easy to eat meat but difficult to eliminate everything else especially sweets.

Burgers with butter, bacon in the smoker. That's my new happy life as a permanent carnivore.

Has God turned off the spout? I thought it was endless but now it seems to have stopped. Good.

You transitioned to the new life, you've crossed the great divide, now look up not back, aye.

Preface to
FRENEMY TYRANT

Preface to
FRENEMY TYRANT

*Withdraw from the world, seek peace and pursue it, commit
plans to the Lord and you'll have it.*

The family as system splits between the scapegoat and the narcissist with
flying monkey backup.

We mal-adapt to our environment and that becomes the mental illness we have
to heal from.

The biggest mal-adaptation of the wife of the alcoholic is to get drunk herself,
blamed to hell.

I don't care how insane you got adapting to rot it's water under the bridge: you
were just a tot.

Are you still masochistically attracted to men who are only into themselves,
never reaching out?

You get use to getting no attention so the first one who does sweeps you off
your feet tho' a skuzz.

This comes from trauma, thinking you can change him. If only you're nice
enough or a good friend.

*If they don't understand you anyway and then they hear s*it they fill their cup
with it. KK on twits*

DUNNING-KRUGER EFFECT

It's the Dunning-Kruger Effect of the dumb thinking they're smart. Dealing with
this is an art.

They're sure they're right cuz it's what they heard and everyone else thinks it
too: that's the herd.

Preface FRENEMY TYRANT

They're like anybody's family: prodigal sons, miscreants, wrong mate selectors, treachery.

They don't want an apology, they want public humiliation. Calumny, opprobrium.

God, because You are One who puts down my enemies it is You I will worship today/always.

WOMEN GET HIT MEN

It was like getting hit men to do her dirty work. Just gossiping to the wrong person is dangerous.

I got used to constant misjudgment by inferiors in control and it was depressing ya' know.

Legends good/bad die hard in families. Sometimes you just gotta relocate to be yourself today.

Playing victim is the modern curse. Other than that it's all about her and these aren't queenly sir.

Let God vindicate you for you are His and He always takes care of/avenges His champions.

Water under the bridge that's all. You had a demon and you learned what happened, now let it go.

THE QUEEN HATES THE COLD

She who is most sensitive to contradiction will go most crazy with mixed signals/cold situations.

Materialism, social media & reality TV were triple threats turning everyone into narcissists.

Healthy background: Safety, tools/resources, parents healed from trauma, discipline but love.

Preface FRENEMY TYRANT

Withdraw from evil and do good. Seek peace and pursue it. Commit plans to Him, you've won.

When it comes to swindlers no one's worst than the virtue signalers/the continuous one-uppers.

"Be like us because we are good people". That's all we heard from the young royals, so dull.

CLOWNS RUNNING THE CIRCUS

The clowns are running the circus. Now they're saying men get pregnant and they're serious.

Years of false accusation/being looked down upon: things have reversed, I'm on top now.

Stay close to God with Christian restraint cuz things can change suddenly and you're up a creek.

All I know after all these years is good is rewarded and bad is punished by your Father the Lord.

Instead of feasting on your success day try fasting with it: as a cornucopia alights it's higher ok.

A fifty year project done in one half hour. It's like ocean going thru my veins feeling God's power

Their clear move is saying we're the violent ones. They always accuse us of what they're doin'.

YOUR SUCCESS/THEIR COMFORT ZONE

You standing out destroys their comfort zone. It's homeostasis: maintain the system as known.

Life is a ladder and I came from way down there. Don't think back because it acts like an anchor.

Some are damaged forever as memory locks in the cells and muscles like the event is here/now.

Pisces feel things on deep spiritual levels so triple Pisces, get busy and reject the devil.

Freedom [to sin] is not freedom but slavery: tho' it seems like independence one isn't happy.

BROKEN CONSCIOUSNESS DEVALUES

Broken consciousness is a sense of decreasing value. For a woman it's the end and it's terrible.

With a decreasing sense of value, she chases. That stunts her more in embarrassing phases.

Heal thyself: plan to get out. Just that alone sets the brain in a new direction powered by God.

The mere decision collects data needed to escape. You'll be surprised at God's clever ways.

Refusing to know God they soon didn't know how to be human [man or woman] either. Romans 1: 26

Massive identity confusion: men behaving like women and visa versa--of course she chases ya.

THE CHASING FEMALE

To chase is to misrepresent/dishonor herself. Hearing the clock ticking she welcomes hell.

Chasing pacifies in the moment without the existential experience of being desired and sought.

A woman who chases is convinced her value is too low to expect to be pursued: its an undertow.

Preface FRENEMY TYRANT

The whole ecosystem of the relational process is thrown into a whirlwind when she chases ok.

He pursues, she approves. He pursues more, she approves more until connection is true.

Chasers are treated as game and never honored as the prize. You're just a fish in the net, aye.

To "catch" a man is to grasp and control him and what is her bait? It's been sex from the beginning.

A man is not impressed [enough to get on the hook] by anything other than sex so that's the gist.

CHASE & CATCH: MORALS VANISHED

Chase and catch: a chasing woman must potentially disregard her morals in order to catch.

He pursues, she approves. You can get him temporarily hooked through sex but it won't continue.

Out of natural order, you chase/catch but how to maintain a mismatch? Think on this lass.

She has to disregard her morals, disrespect her virtue and dishonor her body to catch at all.

Fact: A woman who chases is reduced to using sex cuz to chase but not catch looks foolish.

Here's the problem: when a woman has sex she wants to bond [get closer] just as he dumps her.

He's pretty good at what he does, she calls it love and a soul tie develops: kept low with him above.

She wants to get closer but he wants his space. Post-orgasmic withdrawal is next always.

Preface FRENEMY TYRANT

He wants space until invested, which happens in the pursuit but that's not happening too.

The chasing female is broken from previous traumas so the bait she uses bites her in the butt.

He pulls away cuz men bond in pursuit. When not given that opportunity he wants space not you.

Every man is attracted sexually on some level but to attract a man is not attaching one.

ARROGANCE OF THE CATCH

The only way she can attach is to sacrifice her body but a man is attached to virtue not immorality.

Virtue in the eyes of the man is "wife swag". The slut is a virtual nobody and potentially a nag.

Virtue's cost is high above rubies--it's gonna cost him something--so then it's appreciated see.

Women should study men: how they think and act. Not impose themselves with a Diva Complex.

When an arrogant female embarrasses you cuz she's so out of order that's the Diva Disorder.

The female narcissist can't see her Diva Complex. It's even attractive to some despite bad effects.

You're so dam arrogant, shut the fruit up. That's what we all think when we hear those broads.

Talking loud and arrogant, standing out or interrupting, using superior sarcasm: that's them man.

She's a fake humanitarian/feminist, a social climber abusing her celebrity in the royal family.

Preface FRENEMY TYRANT

How life works: if friends you disconnect they may not be there when you come back in fact.

ERA OF MISJUDGMENT

In that era I felt severely misjudged every minute--had to achieve a better carriage to be above it.

You get used to misjudgment and it's a guarded, lower state. I'd smoke pot in my room to elevate.

I got the opportunity to see what it's like. Being hated by one then the whole group joins in, aye.

Having suffered boundary and moral collapse I know what it's like in fact: your world goes black.

Misjudged constantly, seeing inferiors placed ahead of me: I got used to it and I'm a whitey.

Re-elevate, adjust your mood today: see experience as self-achieved and enjoy every minute ok.

WARZONE CITIES/DENIAL OF FALLACY

Liberals think we're all good/anything bad is justified by childhood: empty prisons/love the hoods.

Democrat's pro-criminal policies have made warzone cities and still liberals are blind to fallacy.

Their jokes stink but when the audience objects they just blame Trump supporters see.

They say "join Biden" in open borders, abortions up to birth, inflation, killing energy independence.

Those who've sold out to evil are weak. Coming from weak families they're sad/desperate see.

Preface FRENEMY TYRANT

Once a group is maligned by the leader you can do anything you want to them, it's ok sir.

You could take a Jew's cow, you could disrobe his wife in public and chase her all around.

This is so incredibly dangerous and white conservative Christians are the target of this set up.

They said it: their main enemy are republicans, veterans, gun owners, election questioners.

It was a speech of a dictator--in style, visuals, words--in Biden's Enemies of the State speech.

SPEECH CHALLENGES ORTHODOXY

The purpose of science is to challenge orthodoxy and dogma but that's exactly what is banned.

They criminalize dissent--weaponizing the legal--and redefine half of us as a national security threat.

A plumber has to pay for your education to make more money: is this fair? Liberal baloney.

Since Biden, illegal got-aways number 4 million so how is the border closed like they're sayin'?

Intellectual honesty and consistency is not something the left cares about: it's frustrating for us.

A group takes power, goes after foes with legal force then criminalizes all opposition of course.

We're becoming like the 3rd world: no rule of law, all is politicized and opponents are criminalized.

The very idea that you can solve race obsession with more race obsession is a terrible notion.

THE CREATIVE ACT

The elder's last journey is a vision quest cuz he doesn't have that many wonderful minutes left.

Your work stands on it's own--you don't have to go out there and defend it unless its poorly done.

They explain in long treatises what the silly painting meant. It should stand on its own friend.

The Creative Act has been birthed, I've returned to a child like at first--from this work I've divorced.

Having given birth I await the LINK to success. It's how it works according to Koestler on genius.

With completion I still put things into place and eliminate what doesn't belong: all upward now.

I've done my best and I've gone over it again, again and once more. I'm done, so light I could soar.

Retirement is like being a child again: psychosis, cosmic consciousness and infantilization.

Aliesthenic hunger turn off: When the micronutrients [not calories] reach a level the hunger's gone.

If food makes you choke why ever eat it? It's the new 3rd category of ED: just smoothies/juice it.

A million die in sleep from choking each year. Since it isn't always discerned it's surely far more.

GO INSIDE INSTEAD

Turn it all off and stop filling your head with lesser things than what God put in there instead.

Preface FRENEMY TYRANT

Superior thoughts are in you already so why distract from those with inferior past times/studies?

You get on a tangent and suddenly the whole day's gone. Brain tracked, self-esteem down.

She's your greatest booster, inadvertently. You excelled to dispel her public shaming constantly.

FRENEMY TYRANT

FRENEMY TYRANT

I'm doing it all day from morn: the specific purpose for which I was born.

I have to do what I do--I can't do anything else, and if tangential I always return to God and self.

I'm so glad I finally found my niche. It's automatic after falling into a ditch/surviving the witch.

No place on earth can supersede the inner realm. Imagine that--you never have to travel again.

We're all busy but if we take time to yoke up with Christ our load is lightened, that's the gist.

Wicked are greedy, that's reality. The best is as a brier, the most upright sharper than a thorn, truly.

Trust ye not in a friend, put no confidence in a guide: a man's enemies are in his own home beside.

Stop feeling remorse over past sins repented of. God doesn't wanna hear about such things love.

Jesus Christ died so your sins could be erased, so it's far better not to think of them in any case.

By being rejected and sequestered you built character and they didn't. Born with a silver spoon = idiots.

FRENEMY TYRANT

She's on your turf competing with you. That's just her script but what is she doing there, fool?

Why be so involved socially--people die or move away. Then all that time invested, for what I say?

Don't feel empty cuz you're lonely, separation means HOLY and now God will in-fill with things lovely.

It wasn't you, it was the devil in you being weak but now you're nice and sleek, forget it/just seek.

Wounded and scorned woman was gone, now beaming princess won.

Sleeping beauty had an evil mother and two jealous sisters. Until saved by her prince life was bitter.

It takes an older female to not accept society's normalization of things--that is her function for free.

It's not what he said, it's the implications of what he said.

The stronger the spirit the more obdurate the denial until they can accept it and then it's gone, final.

Of all input the best is thought. Use all media to trigger it though they will call you nuts.

A bad event occurs and we punish ourselves for life. That's psychology, the etiology of strife.

All you wanted was to love em which they made impossible turning it into fear: family and peers.

FRENEMY TYRANT

It's the most sensitive who get hurt the most in this cruel world like their spirit's killed forever.

Hate, guilt and fear. And the guilt and fear brings more hatred until reality: you can see forever.

Sell your soul--time, energy, money--for supposed protection when there's only One with that function.

The most sensitive are hated as they react and the others are "flat".

Stop seeking love and approval from people cuz they die, move away, cause upheaval. It's God vs. evil.

Whatever you've done, repent then forget it now! Jesus erases your sins, just think of that: wow!

Right before completion you find yourself alone. That's how it always works, it's etched in stone.

Denial is our illness. Evil people exist but our connection shows Stockholm Syndrome blindness.

You're alone cuz God separated you from the evil herd. It's the latter days: people are mean and hard.

Don't say they're nice just to get along. You don't need them, the evil throng.

The mark of a superior chat is how many don't come back. People hate the truth, that's a fact.

Many waste their whole lives in a lie.

FRENEMY TYRANT

Watch who enters your house. They leave spirits and you'll find yourself arguing after the louse.

They don't suicide because of the phobic culture but rather their own sin/insanity in a spiritual war.

The insecure will absorb the sick culture and become the worst of the lot. It's all for approval, A LOT

The hypersensitive is so shocked by modern intrusion they become psychotic/stuck in delusion.

God tells us to hate all evil even if we have it in us, people.

You were too good for them and that's the whole problem. Recall that it's evil getting recognition.

They don't know who you are, they walked you by. That's cuz the good are hated more every day.

The pain you went through, ok we got it. All have it so now forget it--grateful for the gospel, speak it.

Settle old doubts, draw loose ends together: see similar patterns in the past and the implications at last.

Your own talent goes beyond your personal path or the things you went through. Let em go: renew.

If you don't fit you don't feel legit. That must be overcome to get to God's power, to be positively LIT!

Protect the patient from fear. Keep from all bad associations.

FRENEMY TYRANT

A thinker resolves contradictions while the others stay crazy with bad affections.

Letting everything-you-went-through go brings a bright new vista. No one will ever recall it in ya.

Settle all doubts then connect the dots. Then let it all go for you have more work to do for God.

Letting it all go, you see: it was all just a template to create thee but it wasn't for free and was a tragedy.

No one would ever know it, so why tell em? Let it all go now and grow up beyond playing the victim.

Once you stop telling em your history you can say "no man knows my history".

Don't be a sensual devil. Carnal is a black cloud and sinners are disheveled.

Superior man stands high above other men. The problem is lopping off heads: "you're no better than".

They are consumed by darkened minds. It's rhetoric, empty and theoretical, memorized rote, unrefined.

Enough of the movies and outer entertainment. Time to get into your own movie: the eternal moment.

Gotta do it, not much time left. What you've prepared for all your life and which God has blessed.

Enough movies, time to get back into music and think. What is the major point? Find synchronistic.

Separate means HOLY. God made you that tway so stay AWAY.

FRENEMY TYRANT

Forget all of your details and go eternal. Let it all go (but what you learned) as if it was just a fable.

When you find your groove you'll want to do nothing but work, to move, to influence the group.

The only way you can help the group is to not be a part of the social hypnotic, the set-up, the scoop.

We must forget the hurt from humans who are now dead, sick, ineffectual or can't remember it instead.

Nothing--ever--will give you as much pleasure as just your own work. Find out what it is then the perks.

Find your predestined groove even tho' a lost art or never seen before--it's unique and never a chore.

Don't belabor the past or miss the present. It's an energy budget: in memory the moment's spent.

Why remember the era of sin/occult. It's easy to slip into but now you're free, you've repented/out.

Dangerous detours are made in life cuz you don't know what to think then decades go by in a stink.

I asked my heart in the light, which of these sects are right? Chest burning, I moved into the blight.

There comes a point where no movie, music, or person can fix it. Then you go inside and find you're it.

Old templates [social hypnotics] remain in the head tho' the system's dead and that's neurosis, period.

FRENEMY TYRANT

Repetition brings boredom but creativity is constantly clever, part of nature and God's kingdom.

Don't repeat experience to avoid the void. Keep moving, evolving, ever-changing, employed.

Forget what you went through--the template on the potter's wheel: to adapt you became genteel.

Find the beginning and the Creative Act will finish itself. Work when you feel like it, be yourself.

When creative well runs dry there's sin involved: It blocks/we devolve.

Letting everything-you-went-through go brings a bright new vista. No one will even remember it, sistah.

It's not that I don't wanna see you, our paths just don't cross. Save that, I'm busy being the boss.

They're not superior cuz they're social. Get that outa you head, it's better to go inside with God ya know.

The introvert has low self-esteem in a social world. Everything is opposite from truth, inner is the goal.

So tired of cum-bay-ya social chat, how you been, smiling like a Cheshire cat.

Yak, yak, yak: a total waste of time on the phone like as if there is nothing but chat, to hell with that.

Many introverts feeling inferior in a social world end in suicide when they could had God as Guide.

FRENEMY TYRANT

Depend on people, get screwed up. Depend on God, get in His jubilant flow as He mightily fills your cup.

They're taught to bear their teeth like an angry lion, tho' smiling like a needy social fool always tryin.

"Say cheese" says the social sleaze as he castigates the sober saint just enjoying the aft breeze.

Must know the curse is over, you've repented. The future will only get better because God said it.

Social settings can literally cause delirium in a nerd. It's so phony: mixed signals/feeling slurred.

Don't cry when false props die: all fear dissolves when on God you rely.

Our weakness cues God's power. More weak, more God makes you the man or woman of the hour.

Remember the good, scrap the bad. It's all about what you focus on: joy or sad.

I feel conflict, fear, pain then out squeezes a nugget, a jeer, a phrase.

It's all meant to be, that's so clear to me. But the groove you can fall out of: sin then wait and see.

I just like being with dogs and cats. The socials always criticized me for that.

Separate means holy. If apart God protects you for His work but if not you go dry, pat, mediocre, a jerk

Have NO part in modern culture. Watch old movies, read the Word, love nature, focus on the superior.

FRENEMY TYRANT

Leave human society completely behind and get into the right brain, a mysterious adventure in mind.

Your work goes way beyond your personal history. So let that all go and be swooped up into destiny.

Repentance has a huge reward of right-brain living depending on the Lord.

God is your true Father, you don't have to cling to false idols or frail props--you can have it All.

It wasn't that he was an ass but having no self reflected pop culture (no class, wore a mask).

Events and pictures, pictures and events. In between there is delusion and fantasy, that's my two cents.

The cerebrotonic loves so much order that to live with a mess he feels horror/becomes a barker.

I create the home, routines and home life = Then he loves home and for that he's willing to fight.

Even Jesus was lonely at times. Go tell it to the mountain in rhymes.

It's ok to be alone all the time. That's the best company you can have or you'll have to compromise.

You just wanna think. Crawl up into your attic if you have to, it's necessary solitude vs. the rinky dink.

Stop following them, they should be following you.

Throw away address book/attract all.

FRENEMY TYRANT

They are empty, you are full. They are trendy, you restore the old paths which God almighty in-fills.

Not having to adapt to crud means you're high in synchronicity: magic, fantasy, dreams realized, giddy.

Admit it, you were insane. Now just forget it, Jesus can erase it ALL and that's what He's been saying.

There are many sins but that's one of them.

Many Christians used to be gluttons, sex addicts or alcoholics. It's all sin, doesn't matter what it is.

Don't track your mind with TV, evoke thought with music in no groove but your own--be free.

Is it in riches, fame, food, traveling, socializing? NO it's in Jesus Christ cuz He's real and He made us.

The demons from Satan's world will have a natural revulsion against you because of Who is in you.

Clean sweep--drop all from the past, they act as little anchors to old thought patterns, gross/crass.

Even a few kisses is too much, it's adultery for lunch

We don't talk to the dead. Tho' you think you are it's best to remember their good points instead.

Do things God's way: blessings. Don't do things His way: curses.

You're a child of God not a bum. Dress nice, it's fun.

FRENEMY TYRANT

For if a man thinks of himself as something, when he is nothing, he deceives himself. Gal 6: 3

I use travel logs of Amalfi Coast to clear my mind: a return to sanity, beauty and the refined.

Refinement, enchantment, wonderment, potential, majesty, genius, rhapsody.

Sow to the flesh, reap corruption. To the spirit, life in abundance.

OJ: The fact that blacks cheered his release was an ominous sign of the future without peace.

Let us not be weary of well-doing for it due season we shall reap if we faint not.

Maybe I'm too intense. Maybe I should just go dense, watch movies/forget about it all until it ends.

No matter what your sins will find you out. You can't hide, they'll be shouted from the rooftops.

You didn't kill him just cuz he died after you hated him/wished him dead: how complexes are fed.

A good person considers his animals. He has empathy but the rest are cold, thoughtless/bitter pills.

We're all beasts behind the smiles. Stop bearing your teeth to me, trained to have social style.

Gall: Doesn't know a thing, fishing around hoping something will turn up putting pressure on us all.

Stop repeating the same experience cuz it won't be the same effect. Keep evolving, you're the Elect.

FRENEMY TYRANT

Why does God say to visit the widow? Cuz it's the worst possible thing ya know.

The alcoholic thinks he can take a drink and remain captain of his ship. He can't--it'll be a disastrous slip.

Why can't you just say it? Why long introductions so boring, give us a break and don't delay it.

I have often regretted my speech, never my silence. Xenocrates

STICK TO WHAT GOD MADE

Fruits, greens, nuts and seeds. That's the food for man, all else is carcinogous/fattening, geez.

Pain and sickness: It's the food. It's the food. It's the food, fool!

Everyone loses their looks with this stuff. There's only one possible way: fast daily, it's not tough.

Is gluttony as high an activity as playing a violin? It seems this is a lower desire of gross sensuality, friend.

Hedonism: pleasure as the highest good. Epicureanism: have restraint

If you eat that food you'll look that way--how they all distort after 40.

Creepy subculture of mukbang videos watching people binge on junk, wow.

When bit by the glutton demon one can't stop--gaining weight but not being able to escape.

FRENEMY TYRANT

More agile, awake, alive, insightful, life is magical: clears the brain—fasting prevents feeling insane.

Maintain your cute figure: skip lunch and dinner.

Fake food restaurants: Those who eat out daily or much will get ugly and fat from those haunts.

Food is rife with scams: even coffee, rice, honey and especially fish or meats should be outlawed/banned.

Fake foods are shallow, flat, boring tastes--while real foods are galaxies never before experienced.

"Pure" olive oil is the lowest grade possible. Some are cut with soy and on the body, that's volatile.

The fish industry is the most fake dish: Red snapper is usually tilapia which doubles for catfish.

Lowcarb theory says glucagons opens blood vessels but I just grew saddle bags and love handles.

They mean nothing, you mean everything.

Those who eat dinner choke in their sleep.

Choke to death: "died in his sleep".

Don't drink, it leads to drunkenness even in the best of us.

Gluttony is a sin. We're to cut off our right hand if so inclined my friend.

Nervous gabbing and gregarious gluttonizing.

FRENEMY TYRANT

Tho' marginalized and living austere, we got leaner and meaner while the left became complacent bores.

He's massively delivering and don't forget you're not hearing about it. Fake news won't report/hides it.

College kids have been sheltered, confirmed and coddled and that's why they're so weird/bummed/volatile.

The reverse of this picture is white genocide in Africa: killing white farmers or put in squatter camps.

We don't care about your color or gender we're in this together to make America great again sir.

While we got strong the left got lazy because they've owned academia, media and TV in America.

We were ostracized and had to live in the wilderness. We got strength and wise charisma from this.

The left has lost it's capacity to connect with the American people: No more charisma, just plain evil.

Having lost their charisma with us the left screams "Russia!"

Their next move is always escalation of lies and slander and to never give up until six feet under.

Historically the left always chose to whip up frenzy, hatred and violence against those who oppose.

We need wordsmiths taking the front line in this culture war. Not bullets and bombs just speak from afar.

FRENEMY TYRANT

Spiritual burdens are introduced by the rot they're taught: the traditions of men/rituals for naught.

It's not about equal pay but belittling men, our fighting force--and destroying family of course.

By the way you talk it's obvious you're a sick liberal. Just one word/gesture gives you away by now.

Turn on the TV and it breaks your heart what people are being taught in the name of religion/NOT.

Traditions of men make void the word of God and strip your power then church becomes boring/nod.

Empty ceremonies: the religious thing to do.

Go to church and not hearing God's word they feel frustrated, anxious. But hear it, it's the best.

If we hear God's word and ignore the traditions of men He lightens our load with these gems.

Mankind is evil--fallen--so you just have to stop trusting them and just love God--are you all in?

Hillary is horrible. Dear God how's she staying outa jail? But we the good will be ok, the deplorables.

God brings his children out from under burdens.

Usually God doesn't put burdens on us we put em on ourselves but then he saves us from lush or louse.

The land is full of adulterers and false prophets.

FRENEMY TYRANT

Churches turning things upside down--what's right is wrong and right is wrong--is folly to God.

God's not sleeping and He doesn't miss a thing: "For I shall bring evil upon them". Jer 11: 11.

They strengthen the hands of evil doers so that none can return from his wickedness, like Sodom.

Cull the pack to lift the burden for the others as the Lord does.

Africans dress better than Americans who've become sloppy from the sixties in class rebellion.

If her purse and shoes match she's criticized ("matchy matchy") because it reminds of the fifties.

The liberal hippies deliberately dropped all codes of ethics, morals, dress, order and precedent.

Cull the bully from the pack and everyone gets their life back.

Ignore false prophets: they make you vain, lead you astray, speak visions from their own heart.

The false prophets said "no evil will come to you" just before they're went into dreaded captivity too.

The whirlwind is God's wrath manifested to fall grievously on the head of the wicked. Jeremiah 30: 23

Anger of the Lord will not return (He won't get over it) until He performs the thoughts of His heart.

FRENEMY TYRANT

Truth dispels falsehood. Then like a light in a dark cavern we rise up in town or neighborhood.

The Lord has not chosen these prophets but they run to the pulpits to teach their nonsense.

The thing that makes things right is God's word but the prophets don't teach, they're of the world.

They preach "peace and prosperity" as we go into captivity.

God has feelings and emotions and don't you know it hurts Him to see you worshipping that scum.

Dear Lord I only wanna do Your bidding and if that means telling them off I'm willing. Poli-Psych Poet.

Churchist: You're not teaching God's word you're teaching your own word from your own traditions.

Churchist, defined: It's not about God but your own mind.

Stop prophesying false dreams causing God's people to err. He did not send you, false preachers.

If you don't think it's superior to be moral not a filthy sinner then you the bummer are thrown asunder.

God is fierce with the enemies of His own. I have witnessed this and they're all gone, every one.

They'll have to answer for rising up against God's people when weak--it all comes back to sneaks.

Hippies dressed like paupers to prove something: a total break from niceness and convention.

FRENEMY TYRANT

 **False prophets: Nothing they prophesy ever comes to be.**

They make God's word more complicated than it is to exalt themselves--that's how it is with self.

Once you've seen His mighty works and repent not, things go worse for you than Sodom with Lot.

If you don't know the Son there's no way you know the Father.

Like the yoke of huge beasts shared, Jesus says take MY yoke to get things done: we're paired.

Reverse outa the filthy culture that justifies horrible things and calls it cool, like flings/being a fool.

It is easy to put His yoke on and He is able to lighten you load.

Don't overburden the flock with ceremony and spiritual anxiety.

The Pharisees have their little rituals like water thrown over the shoulder--silly airs becoming boulders.

Phony rituals replace the word of God and then it's all over, the church has become mod/of the mob.

Pharisees clean outside of the cup but inside they are ravening wickedness (which never stops).

You forget to teach people of the love of God and of judgment. The flock's misled from your reluctance.

The pharisees love the uppermost seats. They like to be above everyone else while they cheat.

FRENEMY TYRANT

They think they can buy their way into heaven or get outa any difficulty. Not true, God will fix it, see?

"Rabbi, Master": They love to hear it as they put on their religious show, but Jesus was humble.

Your works are dead (no one's aware of them) and you are hypocrites (stage actors): just bums.

Nothing more boring than the false church. Meetings, petty competitions and never God's word.

If you say all churches are alike you're a fake. You can't see the flakes, you have no discernment ok?

They may have it all but they don't have God. That makes them losers: no escape from being flawed.

Jesus says come to me, learn my ways if tired of the traditions of men--not ever taught God's truth, amen?

We've fallen so far into debauchery we must reject ALL of it, as the Puritans did in our beginnings.

These people are gross, disorderly, disheveled, mouthy, sensual and devilish so reject this mess.

Always trying to trip you up and find a contradiction in God's word.

Bear each other's burdens, thus fulfilling the law of Christ which is love.

Laying wait for something out of His mouth that they may accuse Him.

You lay men with burdens grievous to be born and forbid those crying for knowledge of God's word.

FRENEMY TYRANT

Scripture-lawyers overburdening us with ceremony: bricks to carry and stuff I don't wanna know, really.

Cultural achievement and sexual restraint = correlation.

Liberal society loses cohesion/purpose.

It's true it's all just energy like Einstein said, but that doesn't mean we can't calibrate reality worst/best.

Never allow your husband a female masseuse. A transmission of spirits through touch: refuse!

You're the stupidest wife to allow a female masseuse for your husband. Stop justifying touching sins.

A female masseuse sells services to touch men as they think thoughts and it's all-ok you suggest?

I suppose it's unenlightened of me. But men think thoughts--who doesn't know this? It's disgusting.

When you sense evil taken for granted as normal, separate out and make all such relations formal.

People object to affairs but not to a masseuse. Learn to draw lines to be the head not the caboose.

There are no lines except adultery so when accepted things lead to it they act like its a big mystery.

Since they fail to take a hardline it's a turkey shoot for the refined.

But each one is tempted when he is drawn away by his own desires and enticed (James 1:14).

FRENEMY TYRANT

You say something wrong, they're gone. You play the game, they're a friend again but not one to count on.

You showed them light and they could not attain. They couldn't come up, fill your shoes, abstain.

Globalist plan to weaken the military: lower standards so that women "fit" so we won't have victory.

Our military is about effectiveness not virtue signaling.

Costs astronomical, weakens group cohesion, distracts from main mission of military, end of story.

Youth love Trump and boo Obama.

From "you didn't build that" to "you can build/be anything you want" (Trump)

Too many friends leads to ruin. People mistakenly think "more friends, more protection"--it's falsehood.

Would Jesus walk into such a place and ask for a massage?

Many men feel guilty after female massage for their thoughts and thus it is sin, lies they bought.

OMG: The things we did under social hypnotism, but what is now possible out of mind control!

Men get stimulated by massage that's a known fact/you can't control their thoughts, forget that.

To the social (evil) culture, solitude's a hideous thing. The rocket-launcher to genius they disdain.

FRENEMY TYRANT

They were so cold I felt a drought and heartbreak. Nothing could fill it till God said "awake"!

Most destructive myth: "people are nice". They are wild, sensual, devilish, selfish in their vice.

They don't understand that it's for people like them that Jesus came. Friend of the persecuted/lame.

Cool trendies make a lot of money cuz they play the game/ confirm floozies but will have no victory.

It's about evil men ruling over you so don't say "forget politics--wake me when it's over" fool.

Modern man is callous and crude, that's the schools since the fifties having banished the prude.

Stop using that vulgar word.

They have no lines. Oh! The things they let in, and it effects their looks and speech so unrefined.

You're a product yet an overcomer of your generation so help other victims.

You were created by but overcame the evil culture, renewing old paths which were obviously superior.

They get delusional, mass mental illness spreads, the bedrock is removed as war's waged on the sane.

A cloud of doubt to keep em from being upset is worse than the truth as painful as it can get.

FRENEMY TYRANT

Supercilious progressives have superior virtue in their minds: You're ignorant, they're smart and kind.

I'll tell you why--it's Psychology: Why people act/don't act is the adaptation to family/frenemies.

Adapting to the system setup framed your identity even after breakup--seclude to rebuildup.

Why do you bear your teeth when you smile? Cuz they told you to, it's the social generation style.

The smiling trendy knows nothing so he'll pay you to learn him.

The smiling trendy loves Obama and hates Trump tho' in other respects he seems ok, yet a chump.

The women's pussy marches are no good--they're just a coalition of weakness and victimhood.

The left owns "hope" and "hate" is about everyone else.

Truth is revealed when evil destroys itself.

Feminists hate feminine women.

If you have a "big announcement" say it first not make us wade through boring video, it's a curse.

Bonanza is America's favorite: all about morals, crime and forgiveness.

Arguing with the left is like a rabbit explaining speed to a snail: it's of no avail so save your breath or fail.

With the media it's a race to the bottom.

FRENEMY TYRANT

Get used to being set apart, for adapting to them will bog you down, destroy life and you'll have to restart.

We're two generations at least from sanity, so there's no way intelligence can snap back anyway.

They'd have to have graduate level courses for understanding, but couch it as if for kids, and kindly.

They don't have to like it to be good. People die or they move away so don't take social seriously, understood?

Dumbing down started two generations back so when you talk to grandma she's also a liberal/cracked.

Even old ladies wanna look tough. Everyone's a gangster and it's all fluff.

Gotten away with so much, feel invincible/giddy: Wanna bring the west down/replace with tyranny.

You'd better focus on politics to ensure evil men don't rule over us.

The left wanted that Jezebel (the whore of Babylon blackmailed by all) in there to finish America off.

A handpicked jury from the swamp says this or that and the fake news reports lies as facts.

People instinctively know they're liars.

They didn't get what they wanted so fighting like wild animals hunted

This is the big battle for America's future against criminals/multinationals wanting to screw her.

FRENEMY TYRANT

Trumpism described: If policies make sense support em, but if policies don't support America, drop em.

Realignments: I get chills it's so epic. Record numbers of dems switching parties to be part of it.

The polls are fake--Trump's not losing his base.

Liberals: set up to accept the view but now they're addicted, can't get out-- denial brings drought.

I said the wrong thing and she went away. I curbed my speech and it was all- ok but any trust is far away.

I don't like modern movies, ick! Bad script, boring, ugliness, too much sex and relying on effects.

Modern movies are far-fetched and poorly scripted. They're agenda-driven as politics has shifted.

Military is not a social experiment. 61% of transgenders have a suicide end.

America's four trillion richer due to Trump

They think they still live in the carefree days of Obama-Clinton corruption but will find out soon not.

Schulz is revealing a nasty woman status surpassing her comrade Hillary Clinton.

It's about policies not worshipping of man. If you wanna worship man move to N. Korea or Cuba/be a fan.

Alex Jones and Savage spend time discounting accusations: it's boring always being in reaction.

FRENEMY TYRANT

All this chaos is from scum realizing it's in a big crisis.

Knowing there's a political reallignment in USA, they sell the hoax that Trump's lost his base, ok?

Hoax: Telling you there's an indictment, impeachment, removal coming--that your president is toast.

Crazy California wants to take your car/kill your pets to stop global warming. Insane control freaks: warning!

The Nazi roots of the American left.

It's a myth Trump's polls are down. Science shows him at 60%, big in town.

Refuse to watch FOX again for saying he's completely gone, getting us ready for what THEY want.

They are ignoring the wave of prosperity taking over the nation in record stock numbers historically.

Trump has broken thirty records in the last four months, ignored by FOX.

America's four trillion richer after just six months but fake news only reports the phony Russian hoax.

RINOS, Neocons, elite republicans wanna maintain their stranglehold on us so they hate Trump.

Trump takes reins off of small businesses and RINOS hate that--want open borders/live off the fat.

Bringing jobs back to America while pointing the finger at those responsible like a Wash D.C. enema.

The RINOS and Neocons don't like being blamed for the state of the nation so they wanna kill him.

FRENEMY TYRANT

 **Please let your wonderful president know millions of Americans have his back.**

They'd rather focus on Russia then real news and things people truly care about. Donald Trump

"He's demoralized, he's depressed" so you by extension feel depressed, give up the whole mess.

"Your leader is a lazy slob about to give up, on the edge..."

America is a total failure according to Newsweek.

He's lazy and has failed in everything he has done in his life. Newsweek

Legends in their own minds, the mice that roar.

Corrupt Mueller--so much evil taking Muslims off the radical list and covering up for Clintons.

They wanna keep the creep in there as the fourth branch of government that you never elected.

The dems/neocons wanna keep big insurance in to screw you: truth

RINOS worse than dems cuz it's pure treachery, all about money.

They worked so hard (committed so many crimes) to bring you corrupt Lady President, they unhinged/unkind.

We've come so far but then it's so nasty to see how evil the media is as they all pile on.

Their piling-on only shows their weakness.

A bunch of fools thinking that's it when it's not it at all.

FRENEMY TYRANT

We need those in power to deal with ISIS, N. Korea and so much more but they don't care.

They wanna paralyze the president so if he doesn't accept all of Soro's world operations, forget it.

GLOBALISM AND ISLAM

Americans spoiled by peace don't even know a fence and locked gate protects from the street.

Multiculturalism is white genocide.

They go on jihadi pillaging-raping-killing vacations where they earn bones through this rites of passage.

Left aligned with Islam cheers when whites are mowed down.

"No one is allowed to talk to any Russians"--oh come on.

Mass immigration was a plot to take down the last bastion--the west--against global governance.

To the UN "family planning" means depopulation and replacement populations.

Falling birthrate in the west but they still push family planning: the specter for whites is chilling.

Mass immigration wasn't a reaction to war or catastrophe but what they had all along: planned tragedy.

The globalists want a tenfold increase in immigration levels: way more than just replacing white folks.

The west's bad fate: Replacement for population decline and aging for low fertility/mortality rates.

FRENEMY TYRANT

If you want freedom and political stability you must have a homogenous culture with similar values.

Governments import populations known to cause trouble then expand operations to keep the peace.

Globalist hippy goal for years: switch immigration to the west from white Europeans to the Third World.

Immigration into the west is based on the concept that all cultures are interchangeable: hah.

Shariah Creep is Islamists aligning with feminists to eliminate female beauty.

Attractive thin women are the new victims.

She's arrested for wearing a skirt but the feminists don't care--they're only hurt over certain words.

Signs of cultural enrichment: throwing acid in faces for fun.

With Christians it's an individual thing, With Islamists it's the contagion of madness/the left wing.

It's not about banning bleach or acid but massive uncontrolled immigration and many are rabid.

Somali cop shot the white women cuz "someone was mean to Muslims on twitter"/that's the ending.

A Muslim ban is 100% effective in preventing terrorism.

Black South Africa: strong communist element.

FRENEMY TYRANT

When a nation doesn't share common values an external force needs to be placed to bring restraint.

You're a racist to see cultural differences.

Divergent evolution: different histories, cultures, gender methods, state concepts, religions.

It is racist to "prefer the people who are here to those who are not here."

They're paid to not assimilate: You don't have to learn the language, you don't have to wait.

Welfare state is the best deal for those with an IQ of 80/no appeal.

One group suddenly subsumed under another group over religious differences: population coup.

Homogeneity in a community is associated with positive outcomes: joy.

It's racist to exclude anyone from the country whether legal or illegal: this thinking is liberal.

Diversity plus proximity = WAR.

White man in Africa is stampeded with how he oppressed em but now it's a black majority: scam.

You will be killed for saying things like "there are some parts of colonialism which are good", no kidding.

If this isn't the tribulation, I'd hate to imagine because Europe's gone mad and I'd hate to be them.

If cultural differences fall on racial lines they'll never get along.

HIX POLITIX

Globalist hippy goal for years: dissolve white society by flooding the west with disparate populations then expanding operations to keep the peace. When a nation doesn't share common values an external force is placed to bring restraint. Mass immigration to the west is based on the notion that all cultures are interchangeable and you're a racist to see cultural differences! For freedom and political stability we need value homogeneity.

HIX POLITIX

You subvert an organization by putting people in it who don't belong there.

Groups like Boy Scouts fail when they have a particular political viewpoint, not desire for success.

The thing about the left is that in nothing flat they turn the good guys into the bad just like that.

In the past blacks had two parent families, were religious and would discuss bible verses.

There was no racism and black men didn't whine about persecution and we were friends then.

They could dance and Soul Train ruled! Tall and thin not chunky burly scary mean debauched fools.

Grew up without fathers/family then Barrack tells em it's the white man's fault and they're angry.

Most blacks (98%) literally hate white Americans but it wasn't that way before. Jesse Peterson

The many black preachers talking against whites from the pulpit are no good. Jesse Peterson

The blacks are not free thinkers anymore and don't believe in principals or values, family or God.

It's gotten so bad we expect blacks to act that way and cater to them or be called racist: high pay.

Not your imagination tho' they'll say it is. You're scared of something/don't need to know what it is.

Worst disaster ever: No father/being raised by liberal mothers yet liberals see that as utopia.

It's not about your color or whether male or female but the God you serve. Jesse Lee Peterson

Catalyst: They've been spoiled thru free stuff while leaders tell em whites (Trump) are racist.

Liberal media/dems tell em it's all about race not what's right, repeating same mistakes/no light.

Blacks: destruction of the family, loss of fathers, hatred of mothers and blaming it all on others.

Because they're so angry they love entertainment which drives conflict but triggers feeling dissed.

They hate good and love video "This is America": more than anything else this shows evil agenda.

The video was so spiritually dark and they love this stuff. Think of that, liberals can't get enough.

Don't ever fear them because they have no courage just a false sense of intimidation/evil-loving.

Think black: all the same way, dumbed down, demoralized, persecution complex, acting like fools.

They will never get better as long as teachers, parents, preachers allow em to blame others.

HIX POLITIX

The same creepy politicians excusing murderous thugs are ok with abortion of children.

Instead of God and devil they call it "positive/negative power": no punishments/rewards.

Anger brings despair and despair kills the soul. Life becomes dark, meaningless, mean, old.

Normal people don't defend murderers but the democrats defend MS-13--what, for potential voters?

Obama divided us, weakened the nation, taxes/regulations, took away jobs, opened borders = CHAOS.

Why would the left be defending the country's most violent street gang? Not delusional, lunatic.

After defending MS-13 murderers the left blames NRA for Santa Fe Shooting: how inferior.

I marveled at the royal wedding Christian when the UK is filling in with the opposite orientation.

Homosexuality's not about love, family or civil rights--it's about sex and anger blocking repentance.

Transgender suicide rate: 87% and you think it's great?

80 million millennials so brainwashed they fall for this crap

Donald Trump is not a girlie man and that's why they hate him.

Whites with highest grades are rejected for the wrong skin color.

Blacks are more violent/rapacious but it's pinned on whites who just live their own lives.

HIX POLITIX

Causation: A combination of being insane and extremely low self-esteem in a toxic nation.

He's a straight, white, Christian, conservative man of POWER--hated by those without fathers.

Good man recognizes evil calling it "animal" while left says "they're all good" confusing the people.

That's why we love Trump: he sees it, says it and nails it while liberals never see a difference.

If it's all good would left see Hitler as good? They never answer questions or we're misunderstood.

"Animal": Only the good can see/nail evil while evil says it's all good except conservative people.

Using "animals" to describe em doesn't even begin to peg these horrific hellish gang members.

Yak-yak-yak, blah-blah-blah, all social hypnotism and accepted narratives, what a bore you are.

It's good Meghan can cook but what of the liberal feminist stuff she's spouting like a kook?

Meghan Markle the Queen of Diversity giving feminist speeches but with the old queens she clashes.

What is conservative, really? God-given rights, limited government, personal responsibility.

He's fifth in line so why not split from royal duty to jet-set with Hollywood, and good riddance.

HIX POLITIX

Modernity is debauchery, clear and simple. It's advanced thru platitudes and vagueries, puerile.

I don't blame the Queen for hating the stuff she's hearing, I'd hate it too if it were in my family.

It's almost like it's planned: a half black pretty feminist spouting the lines we hate the most.

You wanna ban guns? Gun-free London is the murder capital of the world using knives, what fun.

If all gun owners are responsible for those gun crimes then all men are responsible for rapes.

Reflected Glory: Blacks *all* married to royalty. Did same thing with Obummer: *all* of em were president.

Unlike a fine wine the Obamas become more disgusting with time--got PTSD from all the lyin'.

You see, I remember how blacks used to be and that is why I am so disgusted with thee.

Told they can't be racist, they get worse. Get ready white America black racism thru the roof.

Identity politics took colleges but also hard sciences--technology, math, engineering: imagine that.

Identity politics: the results will be disastrous for American innovation and competitiveness.

How to attract graduate level students: No one's left behind as we simply lower standards.

What you call "sexually experienced" is just a lack of impulse-control: a slut.

Past Christians broke away from a decaying world so sinful but they don't think that way now.

Rather than setting aside the world and being stoic, churches are like going to a rock concert.

Modern Christianity: Don't question anything I do I just wanna feel good about myself.

National Science Foundation (NSF) is consumed by diversity ideology: it's the biggest mystery?

Identity politics: how science is taught/qualifications evaluated and the results are disastrous.

Evil liberals like Markle put the ideals of social justice ahead of the interests of the people.

Michelle Obama lives off spoils of his position taking more than given saying she deserves em.

SJW isn't even a nerd just going along with the herd by virtue signaling and adolescent anger.

You don't seem intelligent to be doing these angry, edgy "art" diatribes of these SJW tribes.

1984: the past was erased, the erasure was forgotten and the lie became the truth. Stefan Molyneux

All over the country they say "blacks and Hispanics can't follow the rules so ditch the rules."

HIX POLITIX

We're under attack. They've gotten Ireland to kill all their babies now it's one big abortion mill.

We've been led like lambs to the slaughter--this any asinine fool can see, they just wanted voters.

It's a bell shaped curve of the HERD to which most adapt and love but the saints are separate = HOLY.

Catholics are great folks but evil's taken it over.

Even in schools they're banning the word "Jesus" cuz it's a dirty word that hurts people's feelings.

Don't blame it on poverty. People were broke in the depression but weren't thugs out robbing.

Facebook, twitter and the other dopamine manipulators know that the web's depressing us.

Don't forget the protestors of 1776 were Brits! Ha ha the stoic Brit is really nice until he isn't.

At last, UK citizens climbing the fences at 10 Downing Street!

Harvey Weinstein was a Hillary and Obama supporter.

Watching underage images (feeling shame cuz it stinks), end up in jail quicker than they think.

Porn addict: "Always looking for greater buzz leading to a darker place you never believed possible".

They're self-medicating with porn and each time need a greater hardcore hit--more and more.

HIX POLITIX

Meeting old friends again is unproductive because they're all liberals and I'm a conservative.

UK judges trying to ban steak knives--it's never enough for lefties.

It used to be Christians were hardliners against the occult but now even churchgoers don't know.

All liberal labels like homophobia, transphobia or Islamaphobia translates to: "let me speak"

They must shut down the argument in case they lose it knowing it's built on sand. Melanie Phillips

Postmodernism means there is no such thing as objective truth.

They don't conclude from evidence, they conclude first then just force the fit with the facts.

Church lady took in 5 young boys/never blamed em for a thing and they went to prison, no kidding.

You're angry cuz mom was mad & you had an absent dad but you should be unemotional/a man.

Don't reflect mom's anger cuz that's feminine tho' it makes us shudder. Be a man/poise of a ruler.

Men never used to cry, can you believe that? The family relied on his stability/none were fat.

Sin disfigures people. Blacks used to be godly/beautiful but now NOT due to no-dad, sin and evil.

Blacks in the sixties were familial, beautiful, responsible and spiritual. Now it's the opposite, no?

HIX POLITIX

There is no racism, only SIN. This is all contrived to get us fightin' so they can take over/our guns.

It's constructive anger: if we gotta fight we will. The problem is going along with the swill.

The white man is not the problem it's the way children are being raised, the little hellions.

The wicked call the gospel "flat earth" but wait till they die they'll see they're under a curse.

Justin Trudeau has never uttered a syllable that was not a gross platitude of stupidity. Gareth Rydal

It's legal but dam is it a bug so please shut up.

News never tells truth cuz they don't know it, don't want you to know it or been told not to say it.

Many stars sign a blood contract to get famous but later they're taken out when it fits the agenda.

Though they brag these liberals don't care about you they're economic hit men for the globalists.

Our dear leader is too much: He just keeps on winning yet liberals hate him saying he's sinning.

Trudeau is weak and dishonest: a limp handshake, can't trust him, will turn when he gets the chance.

HIX POLITIX

Little boy attacking big daddy? Oh man I'm glued to the tube this is too much, so historic/shady.

Justin was weak & mild during talks then after Trump left mocked strong: "won't be pushed around".

Little wimp Trudeau's childish play has massive far-reaching consequences starting that day.

Little man Justin stabbed Trump in the back as he walked out the door. Tragic, embarrassing, deplorable.

Trudeau's political stunt was the worst political calculation of Canadian history. Peter Navarro

Trump fixed everything then after he left Trudeau pulls a weak treacherous stunt behind his back.

Trudeau threw a torpedo after they agreed--what a betrayal and so weak and immature, ya know.

Trudeau's bad faith diplomacy with Trump then stabbing him in the back publicly: how wimpy.

Fair Trade is now to be called Fool Trade if it is not Reciprocal. Donald Trump

Kim can't see American weakness so Trump must strike back hard as the POTUS thank goodness.

Di Nero said "F Trump" and anyone in the audience who cheered will now have a career slump.

HIX POLITIX

Stunt press conference after the king left. How immature, how low after Trump went so far.

The conservative media like The Blaze have the same owners as the left--wake up about fakes.

Since the 70's good were hated and didn't know why, but then isolation/porn = soul died.

Seeing genders means I'm transphobic.

Admiring man and wife is homophobic.

Those into dignitarian harm have no problem ill-dignifying us on the right, I've often been alarmed.

Trudeau acted meekly while he was there then backstabbed after Trump left and they defend this?

CNN loves Trudeau only cuz the enemy of their enemy is their friend, just like brats or children.

Little man Justin couldn't resist sniping at Trump after he left and liberals see it as greatness?

Trump had every right to push back against this amateur political stunt of Trudeau the grunt.

Now we even Like Kim better than Justin.

Fake news knows nothing of politics. Bad faith diplomacy is a big deal and Justin Trudeau did it.

HIX POLITIX

It takes President Trump's leadership to succeed where others haven't. Kellyanne Conway

People are intimidated by the true man though in movies they admire the fearless men in Bonanza.

Because he was grandstanding he couldn't see what he was doing. Trump will win, Trudeau is failing.

Look at the R-E-S-P-E-C-T Trump gets all over the world. They respect strength unlike us, fooled.

Trudeau made ass of himself in India so tried to regain in polls by taking on strong man of America.

UK has become an evil land where pedophiles walk free but those reporting on em are in prison.

Most powerful country in the world doesn't have to play nice and whether loved or loathed/no matter.

All that matters is they learn it doesn't benefit em to have disagreements with you, the hegemon'

Trump is so far ahead we couldn't possibly calculate his thinking. TV news arrogantly wrong/stinking.

A gang of boys held her hostage in her own house and cops wouldn't step in due to the ACLU!

From their lowminds they jealously see him as a millionaire looking down on/telling em what to do.

The Trudeau-Trump thing has got me so enthralled. It's about good vs. bad character, wow.

A debauched tone came over everybody it was 1990 and it was trendy to be sinful and shady.

Homeschooling protects kids from violence and Marxism. Ron Paul

Why go outa your way to look ridiculous just to be part of a club of the foolish?

It's quality over quantity, forget the masses. Tho' it's great if to God you bring in the most I guess.

The amazing and brilliant Trump video that swung the deal with Kim Jun Un and made him heel.

So to mitigate against sex crime you put out more indecent stuff bad as second hand cussing.

Trump is unburdened by the truth said the ultimate liars: CNN News. CNN

"Any president could have done this" fake news said in another dis while they lose ratings fast.

Art of the Deal in North Korea: You're either gonna die in poverty or be rich with great prosperity.

Once a precedent is set for something it's nothing later to make a mental leap and be wrong.

Hollywood elites worship Alister Crowley who killed his own son in a ritual: these are awful people.

HIX POLITIX

True manhood is strong foundation--honesty, trust, health and sound mind not anger/whining.

Whether your art is lasting or not all depends on your premise and that's liberal or conservative.

To get the correct views from cable news you must invert everything they say. Tucker Carlson

Bashing Trump for enforcing laws he didn't even sign off on, the horrible legacy/leavings of Obama.

Pedophilia is being normalized by liberal media.

It's always about what's good for them not what's right. The solution is to get clear/seek His might.

No angry person can see. They see intellectually but that's a false way of seeing. Jesse Lee Peterson

Kleptos can't help stealing cuz their father is the stealing killing destroying lying conniving devil.

They start the ritual with an anal rape then a demon enters in and that's your beloved Hollywood.

Once you forgive you can see and life is no problem at all.

Forgive em cuz they can't help themselves.

PTSD: going crazy only when finally in safety.

HIX POLITIX

Liberals are posers, they're not real. Studies show they're ten times more likely to steal.

You can't be a Democrat and a child of God cuz it's anti-God, anti-family and anti-unborn child.

The Democrats are godless as well: anti-truth, anti-America and anti-everything good/opposing hell.

Even if they make more money with a family film they wanna "shatter taboos"/push boundaries.

Racism doesn't exist: problem is spiritual, straight outa single parent home. Jesse Lee Peterson

Liberals learn Trump is blamed for children Obama put in cages, quieting the people's rages.

97% black people voted for the democratic party and Obama twice--and you say they're nice?

Rachel Maddow cries: All drama, all lies.

In NYC more black babies aborted than born but liberals only care about babies on the border.

As soon as they had an edge they took everything no matter what we said but God gave us a hedge.

Satan always quotes the bible for you. Test fruits

They're children of the lie, not God's kids. Otherwise how could they ever believe this s--t?

HIX POLITIX

 **It's man over woman and this other thing is disgustin'**

Must tell the truth or children of the lie will take your country.

They spend all their time on social media and don't know how to be men.

Blacks suffering due to lack of moral character and destruction of family but are told it's you/me.

Mockers at feasts or wherever we get together. Learn about the leech then tell the world: speak.

Don't try to convince them cuz the children of the lie won't hear, they're blinded by a demon spirit.

Black immorality due to destruction of the family and lack of character blamed on white culture.

Laura Bush and the RINOS are the same as Hillary and the Democrats so don't kid yourselves.

But now blacks don't have intact families and it's all gone to hell overnight, a liberal blight.

They blame it on slavery 200 years ago rather than the failure of the parents young and old.

Blacks weren't raping and robbing stores because they had morals and knew what was right.

A growing pattern of intimidation, public embarrassment and mob scenes against Republican officials.

Stores and players suffer horribly with their public leftist stance and so will Red Hen Restaurants.

HIX POLITIX

Because Christianity makes you want to do what is right not wrong it is hated by the evil throng.

Liberal's house not built on a strong foundation but sand--this the commie children can't understand.

It's not just a "difference of opinion" but inability to discern good vs. evil or right from wrong.

A lunatic mob is an atom bomb and this broad is inciting restaurant blowups? Black/woman/slob

We don't like you anymore not cuz of your skin color but how you act, justify and demand more.

They will lose a civil war so quickly, but let them start it. Mike Adams

Be honest with them but not angry with them, they literally can't help it. Jesse Lee Peterson

Kids may have common sense but so messed up by their liberal parents they doubt themselves.

Once you decide the people who disagree with you are Nazis everything is allowed/potentially awful.

Stop telling me how good and great you are when I only see petty pilfering by sticky fingers.

Barrack Obama nearly destroyed this country cuz people were afraid to tell the truth even me.

Obama was the worst: far left, liberal, godless redistribution of wealth black liberation socialist

HIX POLITIX

Evil democratic party is anti-unborn child/family/God in public square, anti-military, pro-sodomy.

Blacks in 60's loved God, respected what was right and worked hard, restrained from doing bad.

They're already reprobate if they can't see God in the heavens or political leaven.

The conflate. Taking black violence and averaging it in, saying "America is violence and doom".

Liberals believe blacks are only in prison from racism not criminality so they're released early.

Knockout games--killing old white people. Black cowards are never mentioned now, what evil.

The enormous number of blacks in prison means: "whites are doing it too but not arrested", see?

I love your city, I love your restaurants, but I'm never coming back. San Francisco visitor

Since God gave the gift of artistic/intellectual discernment let Him decide on those varmints.

The left are trained by opinion leaders how to spot you right away and it's from what you say.

Don't you dare give em a break cuz they hate children thru abortion/giving pedophiles a platform.

Though Antifa has been media-fomented to vicious violence they'll still be responsible for it.

HIX POLITIX

Every time you mimic/follow a herd narrative you make a fool of yourself. Neurosis = brainwash.

No way is this a lost cause. We take our power back and it's game over and they've lost.

Pornography is a doorway, it's about brain chemicals that hook the guy.

Now it's coming out through paid contributors on CNN with great regularity that we're Nazis.

With the system-is-rigged mentality you quit after one failure then same cycle for your future.

Fraudulent social justice brings empathy burnout.

They make a big fanfare only to dissolve to vapor cuz their work is a bummer and you're better.

Pay attention fanbase: They accuse the children of God of doing what they're doing, always.

Don't get emotionally involved with liberals, that's how they control you. Avoid emotion/stay logic.

If they say filthy things they're filthy liberals and avoid them like the plague but stay cordial.

Trump's gotten so much done despite fighting with RINO republicans, media/democrat scum.

She's known as Crazy Maxine/Mad Maxine so I wouldn't worry she'll be gone/we'll be free.

HIX POLITIX

Media has lost all its moral authority and what mattered most: their ability to move and shape us.

At this point you will find out who's with God and who isn't. Those who say it's all God ain't fishin'

We take authority over the shedding of innocent blood and debauchery thick across the land.

Trudeau: male feminist caught in a grope. Watch the drama teacher get outa this one, the dope.

Raise your black power fist, it won't put one dime in your pocket or make one good friend.

Black power is no power, what we need is the power of God. Jesse Lee Peterson

While interrupting constantly they accuse you of micro-aggressing already.

May you make millions acting like this but I predict short life cuz it's ridiculous/God's all there is.

God works thru the prayers of His saints.

Arrested in Canada for preaching the gospel.

Smiling all the time is not what this is all about! Life is serious, do His work and be sober.

They refuse to judge as it may "hurt" the person, we *must* judge sin and hate it for good reason.

Smiling preachers wanna be everyone's friend but to the clear they're just phony and sickening.

HIX POLITIX

Instead of hating these crazy people just realize they need parenting and to repent of evil.

If you're not gonna use the bible (the word) in your churches throw the bible outa your churches.

They go to church dressed as harlots and thugs.

If you're a white in Philly you're always ready for unpredicted racial violence. Colin Flaherty

To remedy black-on-white violence you first have to face it but is it ever admitted? Not a chance

They write long boring paragraphs of stuff I don't need to know--no one knows the quintessential.

Ha ha whatever they shine a light on to put us down just makes people more aware of scum.

Never stop speaking cuz they're too dumb to get it--it's for the future when they've woke to it.

Left thinks they've perfect knowledge so should be immune from criticism, so watch out m'am.

Left is aghast we'd ever question the unquestionable so get strong and stand against the rabble.

Not all, not all, not all...but MOST. Jesse Lee Peterson

We are not allowed to talk that way but fortunately our president LOVES to/says it's all-ok.

HIX POLITIX

We just wanna live our lives like everyone else. No one's thinking how to mess blacks up.

These people can do wrong while the good guy's put away. Innocent men jailed for being white, ok?

It's skin color above truth. They portray thugs as innocent children and we see this in Europe too.

Racism doesn't exist. Blacks are in a fallen state listening to liars who get them angry and pist.

We cross the street when they appear not because of their color but fear cuz they're violent dear.

Brainwashed by a theory showing them as morally superior, of course they can't let it go sir.

They've hijacked Christianity to make it into what they want it to be and approve of their insanity.

The left isn't opposed to Kavanaugh it's the constitution they're scared of.

The only way they can feel important is to resort to violence or they will trigger it themselves.

The only solution to liberal laws is homeschool or solid church school unlearning to be cool.

Blacks weren't acting this way (bad) when they had parents but the government wrecked all this.

Democrats/liberals have personal agendas while using black people for personal gain in America

HIX POLITIX

Lying to people, keeping them angry. That's how they do it and it's a terrible distortion of reality.

When people don't have God on their side they use words like "racism" to control you/don't let em.

We must fight this battle with truth, it has nothing to do with color folks. Jesse Lee Peterson

Blacks were betrayed by father/mother--no one else--then triggered/angered by hustlers of race.

Blacks have not made progress, they've regressed back and it's a real mess.

77% of black babies are born out of wedlock and that's highly moral and from good stock?

So the first black president indicates progress? He was the worst ever and the country regressed.

Never put up statue of Obama cuz we don't want to ever remember nor think of him in America.

Why is Trump a racist now but awarded for helping blacks back then? It's all about the money hon'

Trump blimp or pathetic party balloon?

The greatest time in America when evil is exposed like never before and Trump says "want more?"

They get angry right away due to the shock but later say wow that was great, I won't block.

HIX POLITIX

Even preachers/pastors spout that crap: new age pagan religion about we're all "one" as fact.

My "friends" used it as a platform to bigot against me. I hated AA/Al Anon: it's the herd/liberal.

They're all liberals by default because it's all they're taught even in the churches, imagine that.

We just wanna live our lives like everyone else. No one's thinking how to mess up blacks.

Mental revolutions occur suddenly in a mass realignment to a new beat.

These Revitalization Movements have occurred all through history, led by a charismatic leader.

The left is boring, only truth is energizing. Bold words: truth and energy vs. silly tangents: sleepy.

Lawless in their application of their laws cuz it's all about foolish ideas stuck in their craws.

Liberal men are afraid of guns--our one right and rare privilege ensuring life is happy, safe, fun.

Life is no more fun in times of war or break-in by ruffians. In an instant it changes so get your guns.

Just when I think I'm immune to their attacks they hit me again but I'm gonna win this thing.

Since each victory strengthens em no one's safe from their attacks. Most families, liberals in fact.

HIX POLITIX

Liberal social clubs are about rewarding the false positive image, it's a lie and a fake Mrs.

Hate speech is just a made-up term for tyranny and censorship.

They said I didn't wanna get well cuz I hated very boring AA meetings filled with virtue signaling.

They attack us cuz they haven't anything else. No debate, data, facts, logic or history to tell.

Turning affluent neighborhoods blue makes everyone blue and the liberals finally feel screwed.

AA is not my therapy if it's a liberal social club.

It's now a pro-Trump page so if you don't like him kindly leave so a smart one takes your place.

There is no "obvious consensus" against Trump just a mass brainwash and social hypnotic.

Even Fox is going against Trump. Meanwhile they're shadow-banning harmless Diamond and Silk.

While driving us away they're driving the mainstream left's political activists into political apathy.

They're creating a system that will further isolate coastal elites (like uber drivers refusing us a seat).

Liberals please leave, to make room for others more able and willing to learn truth as God sees it.

HIX POLITIX

Leftist cities/police defending people who attack women and children: I've experienced this friends.

"News" used to be reporting actual news. Now it's sitting around in a discussion without a clue.

Christian gospel songs now banned from facebook and our holidays now banned by Apple crooks.

Not only do they wanna break America's back but also teach us a lesson: not just lose but hurtin'.

They hate conservative blacks so they've now banned the sweet Diamond and Silk: facts!

Our boys are going out against these Antifa creeps--our American spirit is now running the streets.

It's only blue cities that allow this Antifa violence and the police are in on it-- it's been admitted.

Trump, please: report em to FBI, get task force against Antifa and stand up for your supporters!

Obama tried to start race wars, knowing cop killings were justified but not saying it (LIARS).

Find the local chapter of ProudBoys and know fifty of you can handle 1000 of those violent guys.

60% of kids in public schools are "minorities" and now the white kids are cowering in a tragedy.

HIX POLITIX

Godly can't be afraid of words cuz the children of the lie use em having no power, only curse.

If liberals can't intimidate you with words or threats they have nothing and will disappear/all wet.

You will make us strong, you'll feed US, cowards. We didn't start the fight but we'll finish it, scum.

Don't vote for politicians just cuz they're black cuz they'll sell you down the Maxine Waters, fact.

They always make two mistakes rather than admit to one. David Knight

240 million crowd together in urban areas and it's growing, feel sorry for ya.

Frisco mayor won't negate public defecators.

Left: Once one starts doing it they all start up--like the restaurant thing or The View broads.

Main cosmology shovedown since kindergarden: we're all ONE (equal) and thus this violence hon'.

Why would you ever go on this knock-down drag-out lunatic show The View?

They've a predetermined narrative comfortable in that studio with a liberal audience: The View.

They can't stand the fact you have real substantive answers or that you've done your homework.

"Everyone knows that" no everyone does not know that, what seems obvious is full of crap.

HIX POLITIX

It's quite different being a big fish in a little pond to being in a bigger pond facing the sharks.

Your vanity's stoked by being a big fish in a small pond but once upstream you face the mob.

They hate him like a fervent jilted lover bent on revenge. Why do they hate Donald Trump I ask?

Free market increases foe's sexual market value and they can't stand that so the fight is genetic.

Censorship in academia is stifled truth in the name of feelings.

75% of the time the established power goes to outright war with the rising one.

If your pastor says something that contradicts the Book why have it at all? Just throw it in the trash.

Engrained in Marxism is envy, so in social generations solitude is the only way to stay free

Why they hate him: It's all about SMV (Sexual Market Value) of Donald Trump bringing hateful envy.

A billionaire has SMV and it's ok if he's black or liberal but a conservative white man that ends it all.

Thinking you're right and not allowing debate is fascism whether from right or the left, same.

Economy is soaring, ISIS defeated, tax cuts for everyone, finally protection but they HATE him.

People are intimidated by real man Trump tho' in movies they admire the fearless men in Bonanza.

Trump is so far ahead we couldn't possibly calculate his thinking. TV news arrogantly wrong/stinking.

Liberals are uninformed, scientifically vacuous and dangerous wanting post-birth abortions.

Democrats ruin every city they run cuz they're globalists: debauched and evil not homespun.

Why go outa your way to look ridiculous just to be part of a club of the foolish?

It's a lot harder to crowd their space and sexually harass people these days, Bill Clinton says.

Trump is unburdened by the truth said the ultimate liars: CNN News.

"Any president could have done this" fake news said in another dis while they lose ratings fast.

I want these criminals stopped, I want these traitors out of our country, I want em off our back!

Half of democrat higher ups wanna have sex with kids. Alex Jones

They've gone collectively mentally ill and they have no bottom/infinitely evil.

Living in a media bubble they don't know what's goin' on.

Have nothing to do with evil and it's a sliding variable but they've gone into full blown illness, mental.

Is this normal, or am I in a bad part of town? San Francisco visitor

HIX POLITIX

To be on the left you have to be hostile to whites, men and heteronormativity so be smart/walk away.

If you preachers don't mention sin let alone hell, how will they know/why would they repent y'all?

The things imposed on us now as everything's breaking loose and there are no lines/SWINE.

Movies are insults to our intelligence: not appropriate for children but too childish for adults.

Silly movies are too much for children to understand but not enough to challenge an adult mind.

We've gotten so used to censorship we accept it but don't: it's criminal, racketeering, discriminating.

We watched our words in fear of their abuse if it was different from the matrix they learned.

Trudeau and leftists don't have answers to problems that aren't totally predictable ideologically.

It's easy for the world to seduce your kids when they see you as hypocrites.

Trump didn't put kids in cages, Obama did that but even so it causes anti-Trump rages.

Why do I say they're immoral? 75% illegitimate births, a no-brainer.

Where did they ever get the notion that this is ok? It's gone way too far into evil, just walk away.

CNN pays for TVs/cable for schools: they brainwash you first then have you write papers on it, how cool.

HIX POLITIX

Liberals are horrible saying kill babies and old people.

The youth are so low hanging on, you know dude, shallow SJW morals and values.

It's Holy Hatred and it's ok to be shaken up and get others to face it too--we've been silenced too long.

We now see that by banning together we can beat you, defund you and make our voice heard.

With sinners in control life becomes boring, uncharming and reckless like Frisco's public defecators.

Those who think it's a predestined groove work all day. Those who say "free will" fritter it away.

Hollywood movies distract us while we're robbed blind/dumbed down by the very same criminals.

I know you wanna kill em but be kind to diffuse the anger while stating boldly on all matters.

Guard mind/eyes cuz once you see it it's etched, unforgettable, horrible and a means to stumble.

Zuck Facebook lost 100 billion cuz we're sick of em and all their censorin'

Donald offered one mil to Pocahontus to prove she's Indian and she won't do it/course we knew it.

Dumb as box of rocks going along with social hypnotics and now can't walk it back/you don't rock.

Evil has a lure--that is temptation, we all have to overcome it.

While the left gets away with murder the right gets the PC guillotine with the slightest infractions.

"Racism" is a made-up word to intimidate white people/dumb down people of color, both suckers.

They lynch straight white married rich men of great power.

The more they go after the president the more his supporters come close/we know the best.

Childhood propaganda limits the practical implementation of adult rationality. Stefan Molyneux

Facebook is a meeting of the minds of people who think like you or who you can convince to.

Telling blacks to fear whites: Blacks are 93% more likely to be killed by a black man in a fight.

Democrats are for workers but put em outa work.

Roundtable discussion with an obvious agenda, that's the news (CNN, NBC) and we're sick of ya!

Stand against the incompetence/intransigence of the corporate globalist media--time to arrest!

Don't plan on speaking boldly for it's gotten dangerous must now proceed with caution: WARNING.

Propaganda is not news.

HIX POLITIX

"Hate speech" is a made-up word by those in power to create division and eventually take over.

Liberals are too dumb to know the difference between "some" and "all"--it's low IQ y'all.

Don't adapt to your kids lower level just so you won't be alone. Be a beacon and teach morals.

Just cuz a lesbian has grandchildren doesn't mean the issue is settled, read the good book, ma'am.

The left promotes pedophilia now, so if we speak out against child rape that's hate speech?

Now that Alex is gone the revolution has begun. Silent no more, it's as bad as Tommy Robinson.

Oh sorry, I shouldn't have said that, someone will make a big deal out of it-- aren't we sick of this?

As we're being banned they jump on the bandwagon cuz they're so weak/have nothing goin'.

The anti-white racism is becoming dangerous and ominous for the future, have caution please.

After Alex was banned we all just left and the whole thing folded. It left a horrible taste, moldy.

Today's left assumes automatically that a brown person is victimized by a white in authority. START

Truth is hate for those who hate the truth.

They want chaos cuz they're not in power--that's the rule they follow so better prepare y'all.

100 KAREN KELLOCK BOOKS

AFFINITY OR MISERY
AGELESS CORNUCOPIA
AMERICA AWAKE!
AMERICA'S DAFT ERA
ARTS OF PALEO FASTING
AUTOPHAGY ON CHEATERS
BACKSTABBING NEUROTICS
BETRAYAL TRAUMA
BOOMERS AND BROKENNESS
BOOT ON NECK
CHAMPION GUIDES
COMMIE NUTHOUSE
COMMIES
COMMUNIST SPIRIT
CONTAGION OF MADNESS
CONTAGIOUS MADNESS
CULTURE CLASH BASHED
DAFT LEFT
DAILY FASTARIAN
DAM RATS
DIVERSITY IS CRUELTY
E-RACE WHITE
EVIL FREAKS (Beyond Gross)
THE END OR A BEND?
FEMALE BULLIES AND FEMI-NAZIS
FEMALE CARNALITY
FEMALE DUMB DOWN
FEMALE POWER DRIVE
FEMINISM AND RUIN 1 & 2
FIX FOR MISFITS
FOOLS & TRAMPS
FREEDOM SPEAKING
FRENEMY ENABLER
FRENEMY LIAR
FRENEMY THIEF
FRENEMY TRAITOR
TRENEMY TYRANT
GENIUS IS HELD DOWN
GLOBALISLAM
GOD USES THE FLAWED
HAZE OF THE LATTER DAYS

KAREN KELLOCK PH.D.

M.S. Political Science, San Diego State. Ph.D. in Psychology, University of California Irvine. Postdoctoral: UCI School of Medicine, Dept. of Psychiatry [NIMH Grants]. Developed the Debris Theory of Disease, a theory of system pathology in 120 books and 22 textbooks for the general public. The theory has a general formula: All disease is obstruction, all recovery is elimination, all success is attraction. The three obstructions are people, habit and food. Remove obstruction and snap to your goals, waiting in the wings.

www.ingramcontent.com/pod-product-compliance
Lightning Source LLC
Chambersburg PA
CBHW061720250726
48657CB00002B/701